this Boss Babe can cookbook

Creole Cravings

JILLYAN ANAIS MOOR

Jillyan Anais Moor

This Boss Babe Can Cookbook
© 2020 Jillyan Anais Moor

Photographer: Sean Coleman
Food Prop Stylist: Victoria Andrews
Makeup by: Jillyan Anais Moor
Clothing Stylist: Ruchi Khan
Hair Stylist: Samira Francis
Behind The Scenes Videographer: Julian Martinez
On YouTube search: BTS Making of This Boss Babe Can Cookbook
B-roll Videographer: Bruce Laureto

ISBN: 978-1-09833-346-1

To my Mommy, Daddy, Baby Brudder, & Gammy:

Mommy: My confidant, My BFF, My ride or die, My boo, My girl! None of this would be possible without you! You have molded me into the woman I am today and damn you did a great job, if I do say so myself.. Lol! All jokes aside, I thank you for being there for me literally every step of my journey.. Through my lowest lows, you have picked me up. Through my highest highs you have lifted me higher! I've always wanted to be just like my mommy when I grow up. I will be beyond content if I become half of the woman you are..

Daddy: My Daddy! I'll forever be your babygirl! You are my first love, you are my forever protector, you are my personal body guard, you are the backbone of our family. Thank you for believing in me, thank you for motivating me. There's nobody like my daddy! I was too stingy to share your peach cobbler recipe with the world right now, but one day I will. Lol!

Dessert Cookbook from you and I coming soon..

Baby Brudder: My sweet baby! No matter how grown you get or how tall you get, you'll always be my little Julesy Woolsey. I love you more than anything! Continue to give this world ALL you have! Go be freaking GREAT! Never settle, always strive to be better than you were yesterday! This world is yours and I can't wait to see you take everything you deserve out of this life and "Moor"! I will forever be sitting front row to all your accomplishments! Always know, I got your back more than your spine do!

Gammy: Gammy Wammy! Thank you for teaching me not to take shit from anyone! I am so grateful for you! You are the most beautiful woman inside and out. Thank you for my mommy! Thank you for being the best grandmother a girl could wish for! You are so strong, you are so outspoken and you are just so cool! I admire you Gammy!

I hope I continue to forever make y'all proud! I love y'all beyond words! Xx

Jilly

Table of Contents

Introduction

If you've been watching my Instagram stories through the years, this book should come as no surprise!

I have shared so many delicious meals on social media. Many of them made up on the spot while preparing them and several I can't even remember what in the actual hell I did to make it taste so good.

Preparing beautiful and delicious meals started out as just great fun for me. The kitchen became my happy place and my art studio for food.

Now, let's be very clear… You will definitely spot me out on the scene at the hot spot restaurants from LA to Houston to Dubai to Europe to South America to Central America to the Caribbean, just to name a few of my travels. If it involves fine dining and signature cocktails, count me in! Please and thank you! And yes I have a drawer filled with take out menus from sushi to pizza. My pallet does not discriminate! In my generation, it's all about going out to restaurants and delivery. No one has time to cook. Well even if they do have time, no one wants to spend their time cooking! Lol

Cooking is in my soul. It showed up, showed out and it's here to stay!

You should know that I was born into generations of loud, know-it-all, can't tell them nothin', Creole women who know their way around the kitchen and are the best cooks ever. And that's a fact! Don't try to challenge me on this one, you will lose.

Growing up in Houston, Texas, my home was always filled with family and friends and of course more food than you could ever imagine. Not just for the holidays, but on a regular day just because. We never needed an occasion.

I would make a few signature dishes, but mostly I was the sous-chef. I couldn't wait to be along side the 2 queens of the kitchen, my mommy and Gammy. At the young age of 24, I've finally earned my crown and we are now the 3 generation throw down crew!

There's a lot of pleasure in serving up a delicious plate of food. Especially when you did your thang in the kitchen and you know it's DAMN GOOD! I love it when my friends come over and I whip us up something finger-licking good.

You know it's lit when the phones come out and the pictures and video begin. I'm like, "Yea, I did that!"

Over the past few years I have created several signature dishes! Thousands of you have DM'd me on Instagram and Twitter sending me shout outs about how mouthwatering my food looks, sending me your mailing address to send you a plate and requesting recipes. I see you, I heard you loud and clear. It's finally all here!

I hope you enjoy every freaking bite!

Bon Appetit Baby!

Xx, Jilly

Bonjour

Morning Meditation Coffee
(Whipped coffee)

2 tablespoons instant coffee or instant espresso
2 tablespoons sugar or sweetener of choice
2 tablespoons boiling water

- In a mixing bowl, add all the ingredients together, adding the boiling water last.
- Use an electrical mixer to mix all the ingredients for about 2-3 minutes. Don't stop mixing, you will see it start to form into the whipped coffee.
- Once it has formed into the whipped mixture, pour over a glass of iced almond milk and sip, sip, sip.

(Note: I prefer almond milk, but you can also pour it over a glass of regular milk, iced or steamed. Once you pour the whipped coffee on top, you can always stir it in with your milk if you prefer.)

I love to start my mornings with prayer and my mediation coffee. It's part of my regime and a kickoff to a great day!

May Your Mimosas Runneth Over

bottle of champagne or prosecco of choice
strawberries
blueberries
blackberries
pineapples
dragon fruit
juice of choice

After my morning meditation coffee, it's time for Mimosas!

- In a glass pitcher, drop in a handful of strawberries, blackberries and blueberries.

- Pour 99% of champagne or prosecco into your glass pitcher followed by 1% of juice of choice. That's how I love my mimosas! Add more juice if you prefer.

- On your drinking glass add a slice of pineapple or dragon fruit for a unmatched vibe!

Fried Catfish with Cayenne Fried Eggs

Serves 4 to 6

6 catfish fillets
eggs (I prefer brown cage free eggs)
1 cup flour
2 cups seasoned fish fry
1 tablespoon onion powder
1 tablespoon garlic powder
1 teaspoon Slap Ya Mama's Creole Seasoning
1/2 teaspoon cayenne pepper
vegetable oil
butter
3 cups buttermilk

Instructions:

- In large bowl pour butter milk

- In separate bowl pour in flour and seasoned fish fry stir well

- Season fish with onion powder, garlic powder and Slap Ya Mama's creole seasoning

- Dip seasoned fish into butter milk then dip into flour/fish fry mix

- Completely cover in flour/fish fry

- Repeat dipping in butter milk and fish fry for extra crispy

- In large skillet, heat 2 cups of vegetable oil on medium high until hot

- Add fish and cook on each side until golden brown (about 10 minutes on each side)

- While fish is frying , in a separate large skillet cover bottom with 3/4 stick of butter, heat on medium high

- Crack eggs right on top of melted butter

- Lightly sprinkle top with Slap yo Mama's creole seasoning

- Cook for about 45 seconds and flip over

- Sprinkle top with cayenne pepper and cook for about 30 seconds

- Remove fish from grease and lay on plate covered with a paper towel

- Remove eggs and plate them then add fish to plate and serve hot

I love crispy catfish and fried eggs. Although it's considered a breakfast dish, feel free to prepare it for lunch and dinner!

After all...who gone check you boo?

Shrimp 'n Cheesy Grits

1 pot of cooked grits
4 packs garlic n herb alfredo sauce mix
(I prefer Knorr)
2 pounds large shrimp, peeled and deveined
1 pack andouille sausage, chopped
5 cups whole milk
2 sticks butter
1 green onion, chopped
1/2 red bell pepper, chopped
1/2 yellow bell pepper, chopped
1/2 cup shredded parmesan cheese
1/2 cup shredded monterey jack cheese
1/2 cup shredded cheddar cheese

1/2 cup shredded pepper jack cheese
1 package ground shrimp (seasoning)
4 teaspoons onion powder
4 teaspoons garlic powder
2 teaspoons garlic pepper
2 teaspoon Creole seasoning
4 teaspoons lemon pepper
2 teaspoons minced garlic

Instructions:

- Cook grits according to packaging to serve 6-8.

- In large skillet, on medium heat, melt 1 1/2 sticks of butter and add in your shrimp, minced garlic and your diced andouille sausage.

- Season with 1 teaspoon Creole seasoning, 2 teaspoons garlic powder, 2 teaspoons onion powder, 1 teaspoon garlic pepper and 2 teaspoons lemon pepper.

- Sauté for about 5 minutes.

- Now, stir in your bell peppers, onions and green onions (reserve some green onions for garnishing at the end)

- Let sauté for approximately 12-15 minutes, stirring occasionally.

- Once done cooking, set aside.

- In large bowl whisk together packs of garlic and herb alfredo sauce mix with and milk.

- Pour milk mix in large sauce pot on medium heat, adding in your pack of ground shrimp and let cook for about 5 minutes.

- Now, stir all your cheeses into the sauce pot.

- Season sauce with 1 teaspoon Creole seasoning, 2 teaspoons garlic powder, 2 teaspoons onion powder, 1 teaspoon garlic pepper and 2 teaspoons lemon pepper.

- Stir well until all cheeses are melted into the sauce.

- In the bigger pot, merge all ingredients together including butter from shrimp and sausage sauté.

- Simmer on low for 10 minutes, stirring occasionally.

- Once grits have cooked, whisk in remains 1/2 stick of butter.

- Pour grits in large serving dish and top with the shrimp and sausage sauce. Sprinkle remaining green onions all over.

I may be biased, but this is THE BEST shrimp 'n grits I have ever had in my entire life! It's so delicious, if I do say so myself! I promise you'll be going back for more!

Sweet Honey Bacon and Butter Biscuits

For Sweet Honey Bacon

bacon*
brown sugar
honey
black pepper

I personally like the thick cut bacon, because it doesn't shrink as much when cooked in the oven.

Instructions:

- Preheat oven to 400°
- Using a baking sheet, line it with foil. (I do this so it's less mess for me to clean up once my bacon is done cooking.)
- Sprinkle brown sugar and black pepper evenly across the foil, covering everywhere the bacon will lay.
- Place bacon strips on top of brown sugar and pepper.

- Now sprinkle more brown sugar and black pepper on top of the bacon.
- Next, lightly drizzle honey across all of the bacon stripes in a zig zag manor going from left to right.
- Place bacon in oven for about 16 minutes or until crispy to your liking. (Make sure you keep an eye out so bacon doesn't over cook.)

Buttermilk Honey Biscuits

2 and 1/2 cups all-purpose flour
1 1/2 tablespoon baking powder
1/2 teaspoon baking soda
1 teaspoon kosher salt
1 teaspoon sugar
1/2 cup (1 stick) unsalted butter, very cold
and cut into tiny cubes *(refrigerate until ready to use)*

1 1/2 cups cold buttermilk
2 1/4 teaspoons honey
Topping: 2 tablespoons melted butter + 1
tablespoon honey mixed together

Instructions:

- Preheat oven to 425°F

- In a large food processor whisk together your flour, baking powder, baking soda sugar and salt.

- Whisk until ingredients look evenly distributed.

- (Note: As your whisking and mixing your ingredients, never over mix. Your biscuits will turn out tough.)

- Add the cubed butter by pulsing several times in the processor.

- Continuing pulsing until crumbs form.

- Now pour your crumbly mixture into a large mixing bowl.

- Next, pour 1 cup of buttermilk on top, followed by the honey.

- Stir everything together until just about evenly mixed (again, do NOT over mix the dough.)

- Place the dough on a lightly floured surface.

- Using your hands, gently shape it into a semi rectangular form.

- Now, fold one side into the center, then fold the other side into the center.

- Turn the dough so it's long horizontally. Gently flatten and repeat the folding steps again.

- One final time, turn the dough so it's long horizontally. Gently flatten and repeat the folding for the last time.

- Using a rolling pin, gently roll the dough out until it's about an inch thick.

- Cut into about 3-inch circles.

- Continue rolling using any scraps until you have about 9-10 biscuits.

- Place biscuit mixture into a cast iron skillet or a lightly greased baking sheet.

- Make sure your biscuits are touching side by side so that they can rise vertically beautiful.

- With the remaining buttermilk, brush the tops of your biscuits.

- Place in oven for about 15 minutes or until biscuits are golden brown.

- Once biscuits have finished baking, remove them from the oven and brush with the melted butter and honey mixture.

Honey, Honeeeey! You can never go wrong with some biscuits and bacon, but pshhhh.. After you taste these homemade buttermilk biscuits and sweet honey bacon, you won't ever go back to basic bacon and biscuits in a can!

Breakfast Goulash

Serves 4-6

1 bag rice (I prefer boil in bag)
6 brown eggs
1/2 package turkey sausage, chopped
1/4 green bell pepper, chopped
1/4 red bell pepper, chopped
1/4 yellow bell pepper, chopped
1/4 orange bell pepper, chopped

1/4 red onion, chopped
onion powder
garlic powder
ground black pepper
Tony Chachere's
butter

Instructions:

- Boil rice as instructed on packaging.

- In a bowl, whisk together your eggs, 1/2 teaspoon black pepper and 1 teaspoon Tony Chachere's.

- I love to use my Wok for this recipe. No need for any other skillets!

- First things first, melt 1/2 a stick of butter in the Wok to coat the bottom of it.

- Add in all your peppers and onions. Stir and let simmer for about 2 minutes.

- Next, stir in your sausage. Let simmer for about 3-4 minutes (or until sausage is slightly crisp).

- Now, add in your boiled rice followed by 1/2 stick of butter, 1 tablespoon onion powder, 1 tablespoon garlic powder, 1 teaspoon black pepper, 1 teaspoon Tony Chachere's.

- Finally add in your whisked eggs. Stir mixture together until eggs are completely cooked.

Optional add salt to taste, I personally do not use salt for this dish. It simply doesn't need it in my opinion.

You can enjoy this goulash by itself, with homemade biscuits, with a fried egg on top, or even quail eggs (as pictured). Once you get this recipe down, you can't do any wrong how you serve it!

Twerkin' Breakfast Tacos

Makes about 8 tacos

1/2 pack turkey sausage, chopped
8 stripes bacon, chopped
10 brown eggs
flour tortillas
1/4 yellow bell pepper, chopped
1/4 red bell pepper, chopped
1/4 green bell pepper, chopped
1/4 orange bell pepper, chopped
1/4 red onion, chopped

black pepper
Tony Chachere's
onion powder
garlic powder
shredded pepper jack cheese
picante sauce
butter
salt

Instructions:

- Cook bacon how you prefer. Once cooked, crumble into small, medium pieces and set aside.

- In a mixing bowl, whisk together your eggs, 2 teaspoons black pepper, 2 teaspoons Tony Chachere's and salt to taste.

- In a large skillet, melt 1/2 stick of butter on medium heat.

- Toss in your chopped bell peppers and red onions, along with 1 teaspoon garlic powder and 1 teaspoon onion powder. Stir everything so that it is all well mixed.

- Allow ingredients to simmer for about 2-3 minutes.

- Next add in your turkey sausage. Stir all together and allow everything to cook for about 4 minutes (or until sausage has a slight crisp to it) stirring occasionally.

- While your ingredients are simmering, in another skillet add a slither of butter on medium low to coat the bottom of the pan.

- Place your flour tortillas on skillet for about 1-2 minutes, then flip letting them cook on opposite side for about 1-2 minutes as well.

- Tortillas should be a perfect golden brown. Repeat steps for however many tortillas you want.

- Once turkey sausage mixture is cooked, add in your crumbled bacon and your whisked eggs.

- Stir all ingredients mixing everything evenly. Continue stirring making sure your eggs cook throughout.

- Once eggs are almost done cooking, add in your shredded pepper jack cheese and continue stirring.

- Once cheese has melted it is ready for serving.

- Place a generous amount of egg mixture into your tortillas topping it off with picante sauce.

(Note: I buy my picante sauce already made. I put some in a bowl, heat it up and drizzle it on top of my tacos. I personally don't like cold salsa. The warmed up sauce compliments the mixture to perfection.

These tacos will have you twerking at 6 am they're so good. Never thought you'd be shaking it this early, now did you?

Pancake Scramble

Serves 1 but big enough for 2

pancake mix
butter
1/4 pack turkey sausage, chopped
2 brown eggs
syrup
ground black pepper
salt
butter

Instructions:

- Mix pancake mix according to instructions on packaging.

- In a separate bowl, whisk together your eggs, a pinch of salt and 1/4 teaspoon pepper.

- In a skillet, melt 1 tablespoon butter.

- Toss in your sausage. Let cook for about 4-5 minutes (stir occasionally) or until sausage is crisp.

- Next add in your whisked eggs and stir until eggs are cooked throughout. Place your scramble to the side.

- Now rebutter up the bottom of your skillet for your pancake mix using about a tablespoon of butter.

- Pour in pancake mix like normal, but not as thick as usual (a thin layer is easier for cooking it all the way through).

- Let pancake mix cook for about 80 seconds (this is so your pancake forms and your scramble doesn't seep through.)

- Then add your scramble right on top of the pancake followed by another thin layer of pancake mix.

- Now flip your pancake and letting it cook for about another 80 seconds or until golden brown.

- Remove from skillet once cooked thoroughly.

I personally like to add a slither of butter to top my pancake scramble off along with some hot syrup!

You are guaranteed to have an amazing day starting your morning off with this dish! Bon Appetit!

Meats & Seafood

Coochié Chicken

Serves 6-8

1 pack of 12 chicken wings
Extra virgin olive oil
Sweet and Spicy Rub
1 teaspoon onion powder
1 teaspoon Creole seasoning
1 teaspoon bourbon maple seasoning (Grill Mate)

Instructions:

- Preheat oven to 450°
- In large mixing bowl, add in your washed chicken wings.
- Then drizzle a generous amount of olive oil on top.
- Using your hands, toss together to make sure your olive oil is evenly coating all the wings.
- Next, season with onion powder, creole seasoning and bourbon maple.
- Then add a generous amount of sweet and spicy rub to cover the chicken wings completely.

- Place seasoned chicken in casserole dish with wing side pointing up.
- Place in oven and let roast for 20 minutes.
- After 20 minutes, flip chicken wings over and cook an additional 20 to 25 minutes.

This is the real finger licking good chicken! Trust me, you'll be hooked!

This chicken will have you singing "Pop that Coochie Baby!" Lol, the song y'all!

Jalapeño Garlic Sympa Salmon

slab of salmon
jalapeños
2 tablespoons minced garlic
1/4 cup butter
olive oil
1 1/2 tablespoon garlic powder
1 1/2 tablespoon onion powder
1 tablespoon black pepper

1/2 teaspoon salt
1 tablespoon Tony Chachere's
1 tablespoon old bay seasoning
1 tablespoon red pepper flakes
1 lemon, squeezed lemon juice
foil

Instructions:

- Preheat oven to 375°

- Remove salmon from packaging and rinse off.

- Personally, I do not like the skin on my salmon, so at this moment I peel the skin off of the bottom.

- Once I have rinsed my salmon, I lay foil down to cover the bottom of a baking pan, drizzle olive oil on top of the foil and then place salmon on top of the olive oil.

- Next, fork salmon all over (that way your seasoning is able to really get up in there).

- After forking salmon evenly throughout, drizzle a little olive oil all over so your salmon stays moist.

- Now, add all your seasonings, garlic powder, onion powder, Tony Chachere's, old bay seasoning, salt & black pepper.

- Cut a lemon in half and squeeze both halves all over the salmon slab.

- In a bowl, melt butter and mix in minced garlic.

- Now drizzle your garlic butter generously over the salmon.

- Next, sprinkle red pepper flakes across the top and add your jalapeños all over!

- Cover your salmon with foil to lock in all the moisture so salmon does not dry out.

- Place in over and cook for about 25 min (that's if you like your salmon cook well done like me. Cook less if you prefer medium cooked salmon.)

I love me some salmon! This slab honestly can go with any pasta in my book, any side in my book, shiiiii just about anything in my book! Lmao

(Sympa is the French word for sexy! Salmon is the best meal that will have you feeling light and sexy after eating! I love that I never have the itis after eating my salmon!)

Baby Brudder's T-bone steak

2 T-bone steaks
1 tablespoon minced garlic
1 tablespoon garlic powder
1 tablespoon onion powder
2 tablespoons coarse seasoning
1 tablespoon steak seasoning
1 tablespoon Tony Chachere's
1 teaspoon garlic salt

1 teaspoon ground pepper
Extra virgin olive oil
3/4 stick of butter
2 tablespoons Worcestershire Sauce
foil

Instructions:

- Preheat the oven to 425°
- Remove T bone steaks from packaging and rise well.
- On a baking sheet place foil to cover entire bottom. Drizzle olive oil onto foil and place t bone on top. Fork T-bone all over (this is so the seasoning seeps all the way through the steak.)
- Drizzle a little olive oil on top of the steak.
- Next, pour your Worcestershire sauce all over steak's surface.
- Now, season your steak to perfection with your garlic powder, onion powder, steak seasoning, Tony Chachere's, salt and black pepper.
- In a skillet cover bottom with olive oil & 1/4 stick of butter on medium heat,
- Place your seasoned side t-bone face down in the skillet.
- Allow your T-bone to sear for about 3 minutes.
- While searing, repeat all the seasoning steps, starting with forking on the opposite side of the steak.
- Once the bottom is a nice brown crisp looking color, flip the steak and allow it to sear on the opposite side for about 3 minutes as well.

- After both sides of the steak have been seared, I like to add a little bit more Worcestershire sauce and olive oil to my foiled baking sheet and then place my seared steaks on top.
- In a bowl mix together 1/2 stick of butter and minced garlic and warm up
- Once butter is melted stir mixture together.
- Using a large spoon, drizzle garlic butter mixture generously on top of your steak.
- Finally add your coarse seasoning lather it on the top of the steak.
- Now put foil on top sealing it around the edges so all the moisture stays inside and you don't dry out your steak.
- Leave steak in oven for about 35 minutes.
- (Time will vary depending on how you like your steak cooked. I prefer my steak medium plus. If you prefer medium rare, I suggest cooking it for about 20 minutes.
- If you prefer well done, I suggest about 45 minutes.)
- Plate this and pair with a nice cab or pinot and dinner is served!

This recipe was inspired by my baby brudder Julesy Woolsey ha! He hates when I call him that, lmao Jules loves a good steak and since most of my recipes include seafood (which he doesn't eat), I had to come up with a recipe to include him so he would come over for dinner. So Baby Brudder's T-Bone Steak made its debut!

One bite and you will think you ordered in from a 5-star steakhouse until you look at the kitchen that is! Eat now...clean later. Muah

Le Bácon Wrapped Filet

1 filet

thick cut bacon
1/2 teaspoon coarse seasoning
1/4 teaspoon garlic powder
1/4 teaspoon onion powder
1/4 teaspoon Tony Chachere's
1/4 teaspoon steak seasoning
salt, to taste

1/4 teaspoon pepper
1 teaspoon Worcestershire sauce
1/2 teaspoon minced garlic
1 tablespoon butter

olive oil

Instructions:

- Preheat oven to 450°

- Wrap edges of filet with a strip of thick cut bacon and secure with a toothpick.

- Fork top and bottom of filet.

- Now drizzle olive oil all over filet (this is so the steak stays moist).

- Add your Worcestershire sauce, garlic powder, onion powder, salt, pepper, Tony Chachere's and steak seasoning all over (top & bottom).

- In a skillet, coat bottom with olive oil and 1/2 tablespoon butter.

- Place the top of the steak to the heated skillet.

- Let filet sear for about 3-4 minutes. Then flip and let the other side sear for the same amount of time.

- Once filet has a nice brown color to it, take an oven proof skillet and coat bottom with olive oil.

- Place filet in an skillet.

- In a mixing bowl, melt 1/2 tablespoon butter and minced garlic. Mix together.

- Using a spoon, drizzle garlic butter mixture on top of the bacon wrapped filet.

- Next, sprinkle your coarse seasoning on top.

- Now take some foil and cover your filet to keep it from drying out in the oven.

- It's now oven time! Place in oven for about 25 minutes

- (I like mine medium plus, so this is the perfect amount of time for me, I suggest about 35 if you prefer well done or 10-15 if you prefer medium rare.)

Bon Appetit Baaaaby! My Le Bácon Wrapped Filet is the perfect main course along side my Crabby Crab & Sausage Rice (pg. 79) or any of my other vegetable or side dishes!

Theresa Gail's Lambchops

8 Lollipop lamb chops (I prefer to buy a rack of lamb already sliced)
1 tablespoon onion powder
1 tablespoon garlic powder
1/4 teaspoon garlic salt
1/2 teaspoon Creole seasoning
coarse seasoning (dry thick seasoning)
2 1/2 tablespoons minced garlic
Extra virgin olive oil
1/2 stick butter

Instructions:

- Preheat oven to 350°

- Lightly Season lamb chops with onion powder, garlic powder, garlic salt, Creole seasoning and a generous amount of coarse seasoning on both sides.

- In a large grill skillet (a regular skillet will work as well), on medium high heat, coat the bottom with olive oil, 1/4 stick of butter and 2 table spoons of minced garlic.

- Add lamb chops and brown for about 3-5 minutes on both side(I like mine a little crisp on the edges.)

- In a large casserole dish, lightly drizzle olive oil on the bottom.

- Next, lay your chops in the casserole dish.

- In a small mixing bowl, melt 1/4 stick of butter and mix in 1/2 tablespoon minced garlic.

- Cover with foil and cook for 40 minutes.

- I prefer my lamb chops well done. If you prefer yours more on the medium side, cook for about 30 minutes.

This is hands down my mommy's signature dish! My dad doesn't eat beef or pork and my brother doesn't eat shrimp or fish. So growing up, finding something we all agreed on for dinner would be a struggle. When my mom would suggest lamb chops, it was unanimous. My mom always paired her plate with a nice fat glass of red wine. Now that I'm 24, I find myself becoming more and more like my mom when I prepare these chops... Except I don't wait to drink my wine once the chops are plated, I drink it while I'm preparing them!

Spicy Stuffed Sweet Chili Chicken

Serves 4

1 pound shrimp, peeled and deveined
1 small carton baby spinach
2 tablespoons minced garlic
1/2 red bell pepper, chopped
1/2 green bell pepper, chopped
1/4 yellow bell pepper, chopped
1/4 orange bell pepper, chopped
1/4 red onion, chopped
1 cup mushrooms, chopped
1 bag pepper jack cheese
garlic powder

onion powder
garlic salt
Tony Chachere's
ground black pepper
crush red pepper flakes
sweet chili sauce
pack of chicken breast
shredded mozzarella Cheese
shredded pepper jack cheese
Extra virgin olive oil

Instructions:

- Preheat over to 350°

- In a large skillet, melt 1/2 stick of butter on medium heat.

- Stir in your shrimp, bell peppers, onions and mushrooms.

- Season with 1 tablespoon onion powder, 1 tablespoon garlic powder, 1 teaspoon Tony Chachere's 1 teaspoon garlic salt, 1 teaspoon ground black pepper, 1 tablespoon minced garlic

- Let sauté for about 5 minutes.

- Add in your washed spinach, lightly drizzling olive oil on top and stir.

- Allow to sauté for additional 2 minutes. Set aside

- Cut washed chicken breast open in the middle, fork the top and middle of chicken

- Drizzle olive oil onto chicken.

- Season chicken with 2 tablespoons garlic powder, 2 tablespoons onion powder,

1 tablespoon Tony's Chachere's, 1 tablespoons black pepper, 1 tablespoon garlic salt

- In a skillet, melt 1 large stick of butter and 1 tablespoon minced garlic on medium heat.

- Brown chicken for about 3-4 minutes on each side.

- Place chicken on olive oil coated baking sheet

- Stuff each chicken with shrimp mixture, pepper jack cheese and a slither of butter.

- Top chicken off with a drizzle of olive oil

- Cover chicken with foil

- Bake for 35 min

- Remove chicken from oven

- Generously drizzle sweet chili sauce, red pepper flakes and mozzarella cheese on top.

- Place back in oven, uncovered for additional 10 minutes

- Serve immediately

This is a random dish that I literally made up in the kitchen one day. I had a taste for shrimp, but I also had a taste for chicken. I looked in my freeze and saw that I had both so I just experimented. Turns out, it was FANTASTIC! Definitely one of my favorite dishes... but of course I say that for all of them! Hahaha
This Sweet Chili Chicken pairs perfectly with my Crevette Fried Rice (pg. 77)

Drunk Ass Crab

snow crab legs
king crab legs
andouille cajun beef sausage
mini corn on the cob
large jar minced garlic
butter
large can of Bud Light beer
onion powder
garlic powder

Tony's Chachere's
salt
pepper
old bay seasoning
lemons
large aluminum foil pan
foil

Instructions:

- Preheat your oven to 375°
- No seasoning measurements on this one y'all! I literally just generously pour all my seasoning on and go crazy!

- Wash snow and king crabs and place in pan.
- Pour can of beer all over crab legs.
- Next, season the crab legs with all of the seasonings (Onion powder, garlic powder, Tony's chachere's seasoning, Salt & Pepper, old bay seasoning)
- In a bowl melt and mix 1 stick of butter and 3 table spoons of minced garlic.
- Using a spoon drizzle the garlic butter mix generously all over the crab legs.
- Now, cut your lemons in half and squeeze all over crab.
- Once lemon has no more juice to be squeezed place the lemons inside your aluminum pan, next to or on top of the crab legs.
- Cover seasoned crab legs with foil. Pace in oven for 45 mins.
- Once crab has about 30 minutes left, boil two pots of water on your stove. One for the corn and one for the sausage.

- As your water is boiling, cut up your sausage. (I like to cut my sausage links diagonally about 3 inches long.)
- Once water comes to a boil, in one pot drop in your cut-up sausage links and in the other drop in your mini corn cobs.
- The sausage needs to boil for about 10 minutes, and your corn for about 5-6 minutes.
- By the time everything is done boiling, your crab should be just now finished in the oven.
- Remove crab from oven. Leave covered.
- Now you need to mix one final concoction for your Drunk Ass Crab to be perfect!
- In a bowl, melt and mix together butter and minced garlic.
- This time add in onion powder, garlic powder, Tony's Chachere's seasoning, old bay seasoning and black pepper to your garlic butter mixture.
- Stir to make sure mixture is mixed evenly.
- Now before you use your mixture, remove the foil from the crab.
- Place your sausages and corn cobs all throughout and in between your crab legs.
- Using a large spoon, generously drizzle your seasoned garlic butter mixture all over your crab legs reserving some for dipping purposes if desired.

Anytime and every time I make my Drunk Ass Crab, there is complete silence at the table! Everyone dives head first into their plates! My mom always told me, silence at the dinner table speaks so damn loud!

Twisted Taco Tuesday

1 pound jumbo shrimp peeled and deveined
remove tails if wanted
1/2 teaspoon Tony Chachere's
1/2 teaspoon garlic powder
1/2 teaspoon onion powder
1/4 teaspoon old bay seasoning
1/4 teaspoon ground black pepper
2 tablespoons olive oil
Mazola corn oil

Avocado salsa:

3 roma tomatoes diced
1 11 ounce can yellow corn, drained

1 15 ounce can black beans, rinsed
and drained
1/2 red onion diced
2 avocados diced
1/4 cup chopped cilantro
juice of one lime
salt and pepper to taste
crumbled feta for topping optional or shredded yellow cheese
4-6 flour tortillas for serving
shredded lettuce
black olives

Instructions:

- In a medium sized mixing bowl add the shrimp, Tony Chachere's, old bay, black pepper, garlic powder and onion powder. Toss until coated.

- In a medium sized skillet, over medium high heat, coat bottom with olive oil and add shrimp.

- Cook for about 4 minutes or until shrimp is no longer pink.

- In another mixing bowl, mix together your tomatoes, corn, black beans, red onion, avocado, and cilantro. Salt and pepper to taste.

- In a medium skillet, pour in Mazola corn oil. Fill about 1/3 of the bottom and bring to a high heat.

- Once hot, place your tortillas in using a tong.

- Once bottom is golden brown, flip tortilla and allow other side to get golden brown.

- (I personally like to fold my tortilla in half and hold one side of it up out of the oil with my tongs while the other side is in the oil. Once the side that's in the oil is golden brown I flip it, and let the other side get its crisp on.)

- Remove from oil and place on paper towel covered plate.

- Repeat for as many tortillas as you need.

- Now line up your tortillas, fill them with your avocado salsa, shredded lettuce, and top it with your cooked shrimp.

- Sprinkle with crumbled feta or yellow cheese and a couple sliced black olives and serve immediately.

What would your week be without a classic Taco Tuesday but twisted style! I am taco lover and I never miss a Taco Tuesday! This recipe will bring a whole new meaning to Tuesday's! Enjoy these Twisted Tacos along side with my Grand Gold Margarita! *(pg. 109)* Oh boy, you're in for an amazing ass evening!

Carmouche Smothered Chicken

Smothered Chicken

Flour
Chicken
Tony Chacheres or your choice of seasoning
Garlic powder
Onion powder
Chopped onion
Chopped bell pepper
Chicken
Veg. Shortening

In large bowl pour 2 cups flour
Roll Seasoned chicken parts in flour
Fry chicken in veg. shortening
Discard excess shortening
Pour 4 cups of water in Skillet with chicken
Add ingredients
Season to taste
Bring to boil stir
Turn heat down - cover & let simmer for about 30 mins.

This dish makes me smile every time. It's Another inherited recipe from my
Gammy to my Mommy and then to me!

It's comfort food for the heart & soul. It reminds me of my childhood and all of
the Sunday feasts that we had. This dish will always be dear to my heart.
I know you will love it too.

Dirty Rice Cajun Stuffed Catfish

2 large bags cooked Rice
3 cups chopped Liver (Beef, pork or chicken)
green onion, chopped
1 green bell pepper, chopped
2 tablespoons Tony Chachere's
2 tablespoon garlic powder
2 table spoon onion powder
1/2 teaspoon cayenne pepper

vegetable oil
8 catfish fillets
1 cup of flour
3 cups seasoned fish fry
4 cups buttermilk

Prep Rice

- Cook rice as directed (use 2 large boil in bag)
- Chop liver fine or use food processor
- In a large skillet, coat the bottom with vegetable oil and heat
- Add chopped liver, green onion and bell pepper and sauté on medium heat for 6 to 8 minutes (or until liver thoroughly cooked)
- Add cooked rice, stir
- Add 1 teaspoon garlic powder, 1 teaspoon onion powder, 1 teaspoon Tony Chachere's and 1/2 teaspoon of cayenne pepper (or season to taste)
- Cover and turn heat to low
- Stir frequently and cook for 20 minutes
- Remove cover, turn off heat and set aside

Prep Catfish

- Season Catfish with 1 teaspoon of Tony Chachere's, 1 teaspoon of Onion powder and 1 teaspoon of garlic powder
- In large bowl pour 3 cups of butter milk

- In separate large bowl pour in 1 cup of flour and 3 cups of seasoned fish fry
- dip fish in butter milk then dip all over in flour/ fish fry mix (for crispy fish repeat butter milk and fish fry dip)
- In large skillet pour in 3 to 4 cups vegetable oil on medium high heat
- Once oil is hot, add fish to skillet and cook until golden brown on each side (about 10 minutes on each side depending on thickness of fish)
- Fish should rise to top of grease once completely cooked
- Remove from grease and place on plate covered with paper towel
- Place four catfish fillets on large plate or serving platter
- cover catfish with dirty rice
- Pace remaining catfish fillets on top of dirty rice covered fillets
- Sprinkle top with a little cayenne

Enjoy!
This shiiii fye!

Pimpin' Stuffed Porkchop

2 large bone in pork chops
1 stick of butter
1 tablespoon minced garlic
1 tablespoon garlic powder
1 tablespoon onion powder
2 tablespoons coarse seasoning
1 tablespoon Tony Chachere's
1/2 teaspoon garlic salt
1 teaspoon garlic pepper
Extra virgin olive oil
4 tablespoons Worcestershire Sauce
rosemary or basil leaves
foil

Ingredients for dirty rice stuffing

2 large bags cooked rice (I like Boil in Bag)
3 cups chopped liver (beef, pork or chicken)
green onion, chopped
1 green bell pepper, chopped
2 tablespoons Tony Chachere's
2 tablespoon garlic powder
2 table spoon Onion Powder
1/2 teaspoon cayenne pepper
vegetable Oil

Instructions:

- Preheat the oven to 425°

- Remove pork chops from packaging and rise well.

- On a baking sheet place foil to cover the entire bottom.

- Drizzle olive oil onto foil and place pork chops on top.

- Fork pork chops all over (this is so the seasoning seeps all the way through.)

- Drizzle a little olive oil on top of the pork chops.

- Next, pour your Worcestershire sauce all over surface.

- Now, season your pork chops to perfection with your garlic powder, onion powder, Tony Chachere's, garlic salt and garlic powder.

- In a skillet mix together olive oil and 1/2 stick butter on medium heat,

- Place your seasoned side pork chop face down in the skillet.

- Allow your chops to sear for about 3 minutes.

- While searing, repeat all the seasoning steps, starting with forking on the opposite side of the pork chops.

- Once the bottom is a nice brown crisp looking color, flip it and allow it to sear on the opposite side for about 3 minutes as well.

- After both sides of the pork chops have been seared, I like to add a little bit more Worcestershire sauce and olive oil to my foiled baking sheet and then place seared pork chops on top.

- Allow the pork chops to cool and then cut open the middle of the pork chops

- Do not puncture knife all the way through, cut about 3/4 of the way, enough for dirty rice.

- In a bowl mix together 1/2 stick of butter and minced garlic.

- Warm up butter, once melted stir mixture together.

- Using a large spoon, drizzle garlic butter mixture generously on top of your pork chops.

- Finally add your coarse seasoning, lather it on the top of the steak.

- Now put foil on top sealing it around the edges so all the moisture stays inside and you don't dry out your pork chops.

- Bake Pork Chops in oven for about 35 minutes.

- Remove the pork chops and generously stuff it with the dirty rice.

- Place back in the oven and allow to cook for an additional 10 minutes.

- Now plate it with some Rosemary sprigs or basil leaves to make it pretty and voila!!!! Your Pimpin pork chops or ready to be served

Chops are delicious with my Zesty Zucchini & Squash skewers (pg. 95) and of course a healthy pour of cab or merlot. #eatwellmyfriends

Pastas

Jilly's Infamous Mac

2 tablespoons flour
1/4 cup unsalted butter
1 12 oz canned evaporated milk
1/2 cup half and half
1 1/2 tablespoons garlic powder
1 1/2 tablespoons onion powder
1/4 teaspoon cayenne pepper
1 teaspoon black pepper

1 1/2 teaspoon Tony Chachere's
1/2 cup sharp cheddar cheese, grated
1/2 cup mozzarella cheese, grated
1/2 cup monetery jack cheese, grated
Salt to taste
8 ounce uncooked Macaroni
Heavy whipping cream

Instructions:

- Preheat oven to 375°

- Follow macaroni package directions. Once macaroni is cooked, drain.

- Add butter to skillet on medium low heat. Once butter melts, whisk in flour. Continue whisking until flour is fully mixed with butter. Let mixture sit for a minute so it can cook thoroughly.

- Add in half of the evaporated milk, whisk mixture as you add in the second half of the evaporated milk. Continue whisking mixture as you add the half and half. Let mixture simmer for 4 minutes allowing mixture to thicken.

- Add in your seasonings; Tony Chachere's, garlic and onion powder, cayenne pepper and black pepper. Whisk together.

- Let mixture simmer for about 1-2 minutes.

- Sprinkle in cheeses (save a forth of each cheese for topping off the dish), stir mixture until mixture is even throughout and appears to be a pasty mixture.

- Add Salt to taste.

- Now, in a large mixing bowl, combine your cooked macaroni and your cheesy seasoned mixture. Stir until evenly mixed.

- Have a pan or lightly greases baking dish ready. (I like to use a glass baking dish and I add about 2 tablespoons melted butter to the bottom of my glass dish and spread lightly to cover the bottom.)

- Transfer the macaroni mixture to your pan. Once your mixture is evenly spread throughout the pan, take a knife and puncture about 6-8 miniature holes throughout the dish lightly pouring a tiny amount of heavy whipping cream into each whole as you puncture it.

- (Note: this is a trick my mom taught me so your macaroni stays moist and doesn't come out dry. Do not over pour!)

- Add your remaining cheese on top, (I like to add my mozzarella cheese first, jack cheese second and my sharp cheddar cheese last that way my dish has that signature cheesy yellow on top.)

- Finally, I slice tiny slithers of butter and spread throughout the top of my dish.

- Bake in oven for 20 minutes or until golden brown.

Now lemme tell you this, my Mac and Cheese recipe will rival the best of the best! It is seasoned to perfection! I normally would only make my mac during Thanksgiving and Christmas, but my family fell in love with it so much that I damn near cook it once a month! This dish is definitely a comfort food, but what's wrong with comfort food? It's comforting, right?

Spankin' Seafood Spaghetti

Serves 4 to 6

2 pounds large shrimp, peeled and deveined
1 pack bay scallops
1 pound mussels, scrubbed (place in colander and rinse well under cool water. Use your hands to remove any debris)
2 jars of tomato and basil sauce
1/2 cup red wine
1/4 green bell pepper, sliced
1/4 yellow bell pepper, sliced
2 garlic cloves, chopped
1/2 onion, finely chopped

2 tablespoons fresh parsley leaves
1 lemon, sliced
1/4 teaspoon crushed red pepper
1 teaspoon onion powder
1 teaspoon garlic powder
1 teaspoon garlic pepper
2 teaspoons Tony Chachere's
1 pack thin spaghetti, cooked and drained
1/2 cup shredded parmesan cheese
1 stick butter
Extra virgin olive oil

Instructions:

- In large skillet, cover bottom with extra virgin olive oil and 4 slices of butter on medium heat
- Add shrimp, bay scallops bell peppers and onion, sauté for 10-12 minutes
- In a separate large skillet pour in 2 jars of tomato and basil sauce, red wine, fresh parsley leaves, chopped garlic, crushed red pepper and mussels
- Stir in fresh parsley leaves, onion powder, garlic powder, garlic powder and Tony Chachere's
- Cook on medium heat for 8 to 10 minutes
- Combine marinara sauce & mussels with shrimp sauté, bay scallops, bell peppers and onion
- Cover and simmer for an additional 5 minutes

- Serve over thin spaghetti and top with shredded parmesan cheese
- garnish with sliced lemon and basil leaves

When I cook this dish, I literally don't have 1 mussel left! This is definitely a seafood lover's dream dish!

Trust me...You will be going back for seconds, but who's judging?
Now get crankin' with the spankin'!

Pasta Pesto Alfredo w/ Grilled Chicken and Cajun Sausage

1/2 cup butter
1 1/2 cups heavy whipping cream
2 teaspoons garlic, minced
1/2 teaspoon Italian Seasoning
1/2 teaspoon salt
1/4 teaspoon black pepper
1 cup freshly grated parmesan cheese
1 cup freshly grated pepper jack cheese
1 teaspoon onion powder

1 teaspoon garlic powder
1 teaspoon Tony Chachere's
1 teaspoon minced garlic
1 teaspoon pesto
half a squeezed lemon
1/4 link andouille Cajun sausage, sliced
4 chicken tender meat, sliced
fettuccine noodles
olive oil

Instructions:

- Cook noodles according to packaging.
- In a pan, coat bottom with olive oil on medium heat.
- Toss in your sliced chicken with a pinch of salt and pinch of black pepper.
- Once chicken is golden brown (about 5 minutes after cooking), add in your sausage.
- Let cook for about 4 more minutes, stirring occasionally

- In a large skillet add the butter and cream.
- Simmer over low heat for about 2 minutes.
- Whisk in the garlic, Italian seasoning onion powder, garlic powder, Tony Chachere's, salt, and pepper, pesto and lemon juice for about one minute.
- Whisk in the parmesan and pepper jack cheese until melted.
- Now Mix noodles in.
- Serve immediately.

You literally can never go wrong with a pasta alfredo! I can eat pasta 7 days a week! This is hands down my go to dish for pasta night! It's simple and doesn't take up much time to cook! After all, who wants to be in the kitchen all night? I know I have better things to do... not really, Lol!

Piggy Pasta Carbonara

1/2 pound bacon strips, chopped
1 package (16 ounces) fettuccine or angel hair pasta
1 small onion, finely chopped
2 garlic cloves, minced
1 cup half-and-half cream
4 large eggs, lightly beaten

1/2 cup grated romano cheese
1/2 teaspoon salt
1/4 teaspoon ground black pepper
1 tablespoon fresh parsley, minced
1 jar vodka sauce
3 tablespoons butter
kosher salt

Instructions:

- Cook fettuccine or angel hair pasta according to package instructions.
- In a large skillet, cook bacon over medium heat until crisp. Stir often so bacon does not burn.
- Remove bacon from skillet with a slotted spoon (that way you don't get all the grease).
- Drain bacon on paper towels.
- Reserve 1 tablespoon of bacon grease in the pan and discard the rest.
- Add chopped onions to the reserved bacon grease in the skillet; cook and stir over medium heat 2-3 minutes.
- Add minced garlic and let simmer for an additional minute.
- Reduce heat to medium-low.
- Slowly mix in your half and half cream.
- In a small bowl, whisk a small amount of warm half and half cream into eggs.
- Add your cream and egg mixture to the skillet.
- Cook for about 10 minutes constantly stirring so your sauce is cooked evenly.
- In another pan add 3 tablespoons butter, let butter melt then add your vodka sauce, kosher salt (to taste).
- Let cook for about 8-9 minutes stirring occasionally on medium low heat (this will be used to drizzle on top.).
- Now stir your cheese, salt & pepper and bacon into the cream and egg mixture sauce.
- Add to fettuccine or angel hair and toss to perfectly mix your sauce and pasta.
- Drizzle vodka sauce on top and sprinkle with parsley and (if you're like me) a little more cheese.

I have always been a carbonara lover! But adding that touch of vodka sauce has made me a fiend! Once you try this recipe, you'll become one too!

Creamy Papi Poblano Pasta

3 poblano peppers
1 1/4 tsp coarse kosher salt, divided
2 tsp olive oil
rotini pasta
1/2 cup packed cilantro
1/2 cup chicken stock
1 cup heavy cream, divided

1 large garlic clove
pinch crushed red pepper flakes
1/4 cup butter
1/2 teaspoon onion powder
1/2 teaspoon garlic powder
1/4 teaspoon Tony Chachere's
large poblano bell peppers for serving

Instructions

- Char poblano peppers on all sides over a gas flame. If you don't have a gas stove, char them under the broiler.
- Once all of the pepper is charred, place in a bowl and cover with plastic wrap.
- Let them sit for 5 minutes. Peel skin off, take stem and seeds out.
- Cook rotini noodles as directed on packaging.
- While pasta is boiling, add two peppers, cilantro, 1/2 cup chicken stock and 1/2 cup heavy cream to a blender.
- Blend until ingredients are mixed thoroughly.
- Slice third pepper into strips.
- Once noodles are done, reserve about 1/2 to 3/4 cup of the starchy pasta water.
- Drain the pasta and set aside.
- Add poblano cream sauce from the blender to the pot, along with remaining heavy cream, garlic, 1/2 teaspoon salt, red pepper flakes, garlic powder, onion powder and Tony Chachere's.
- Bring to a boil and reduce to a simmer until slightly thickened, about 3-4 minutes.
- Add cooked pasta, sliced peppers and remaining 1/4 teaspoon salt.
- Toss until pasta has absorbed sauce.
- Season to taste with salt and pepper.
- Finally, wash and cut your large poblano pepper in half removing the seeds.
- Plate pasta on top of large poblano pepper.
- Garnish with chopped cilantro.
- Add your choice of protein.

One of my fav things about this dish is how I serve it inside the poblano pepper!
I love to fork off pieces of the pepper as I'm eating my pasta!

Very Veggie Lasagna

Serves 8-10

2 cups mushrooms, diced
1 red bell pepper, diced
1 green bell pepper, diced
1 orange bell pepper, diced
1 yellow bell pepper, diced
1/2 red onion, diced
2 table spoons minced garlic
2 garlic cloves, peeled and chopped
1 large carton of baby spinach
2 zucchini, diced
2 squash, diced
1 cup miniature tomatoes, sliced in half
3 jars tomato basil sauce
lasagna noodles, boiled

1 large tub ricotta cheese
crush red pepper flakes
oregano flakes
Extra virgin olive oil
garlic powder
onion powder
Tony Chachere's
ground black pepper
garlic salt
Italian seasoning
cayenne pepper
butter
1 bag shredded parmesan cheese
1 bag shredded mozzarella cheese

Instructions:

- Preheat oven to 375°
- Cook lasagna pasta according to packaging.
- Once cooked, drain in colander and drizzle olive oil onto noodles. Toss gently and set aside.
- In a large skillet, coat the bottom with olive oil on medium heat.
- Add in 1/2 stick of butter, zucchini, squash, mushrooms, bell peppers, onions and minced garlic.
- Season with 1 tablespoon onion powder, 1 tablespoon garlic powder, 1 teaspoon Tony Chachere's, 1 teaspoon garlic salt and 1 teaspoon black pepper.
- Stir together and allow to sauté for about 5 minutes. (do not overcook, all ingredients will continue to cook once placed in oven.)
- Now, stir in 2 jars of tomato basil sauce and miniature tomatoes to your veggie sauté.
- Add in another tablespoon garlic powder, 1 tablespoon onion powder, 1 teaspoon Tony Chachere's, 1/2 teaspoon garlic salt, 1 teaspoon black pepper, 2 tablespoons Italian seasoning, 1/4 teaspoon cayenne pepper, and 1 garlic clove.
- Stir and let simmer for about 2-3 minutes.
- Set aside.
- In another skillet, melt 1/4 stick of butter.
- Add in your baby spinach a little at a time, drizzling with olive oil.
- Seasoning with 1 teaspoon garlic powder, 1 teaspoon onion powder and 1 garlic clove.
- Toss and cook for about 1 minute.
- Set aside.
- In a large lasagna casserole dish, coat the bottom of dish with 1 jar of tomato basil sauce.
- Next, cover bottom with one layer of lasagna noodles.
- Generously brush ricotta cheese onto noodles.
- Cover ricotta with a layer of spinach.
- Use half of your veggie tomato sauce mixture to cover spinach and ricotta. (Make sure you cover entire pan with sauce, don't be stingy)
- Sprinkle 1/4 cup Parmesan cheese and 1/4 cup mozzarella cheese on top of sauce.
- Now repeat everything once more starting with layering you lasagna noodles on top of cheese.
- Fully cover top of dish with 1 cup of Parmesan cheese and 1 cup of mozzarella cheese.
- Sprinkle crush red pepper and oregano flakes on top.
- Cover with foil.
- Place in the over for about 30 minutes.

When I considered becoming a vegetarian, I originally came up with this dish when I first moved to LA at 18. Although my vegetarian experience only lasted one night, this dish is still one of my favs. Even the biggest meat lovers, will be hooked after one bite.

Saucy Shrimp Ravioli

2 cups mushrooms, diced
1 red bell pepper, diced
1 green bell pepper, diced
1 orange bell pepper, diced
1 yellow bell pepper, diced
1/2 red onion, diced
2 table spoons minced garlic
2 garlic cloves, peeled and chopped
1 large carton of baby spinach
2 zucchini, diced
2 squash, diced
1 cup miniature tomatoes, sliced in half
3 jars tomato basil sauce
lasagna noodles, boiled

1 large tub ricotta cheese
crush red pepper flakes
oregano flakes
Extra virgin olive oil
garlic powder
onion powder
Tony Chachere's
ground black pepper
garlic salt
Italian seasoning
cayenne pepper
butter
1 bag shredded parmesan cheese
1 bag shredded mozzarella cheese

Instructions:

- Preheat oven to 350°
- Cook pasta according to packaging.
- Once cooked, drain in colander and drizzle olive oil on top.
- Toss gently and set aside.

- In a large skillet, coat the bottom with olive oil
- Melt in 1/4 stick of butter.
- Stir in shrimp, bell peppers, mushrooms, 2 tablespoons minced garlic and onions
- Season with 1 tablespoon Garlic powder, 1 tablespoon onion powder, 1 teaspoon Tony Chachere's, 1 teaspoon black pepper, 1/2 teaspoon garlic salt.
- Stir and allow to sauté for about 5 minutes.

- In a separate skillet, melt 1 stick of butter.
- Pour in jars alfredo sauce, season with 1 table spoon minced garlic, 1 tablespoon Garlic powder, 1 tablespoon onion powder, 1 teaspoon Tony Chachere's, 1 teaspoon black pepper and 1/2 teaspoon garlic salt.
- Stir and allow to simmer for 2-3 minutes.

- In a square casserole dish cover bottom with 1 cup Alfredo sauce.
- Place 1 layer of lasagna noodles on top of sauce.
- Cover pasta with your sautéed shrimp mixture.
- Pour half your Alfredo sauce on top.
- Sprinkle 1 cup of pepper jack cheese all over.
- Repeat steps starting with layering your lasagna noodles on top of cheese.
- Once you have spread your second layer of pepper jack cheese on top, sprinkle oregano and crush red pepper flakes on top.
- Cover with foil.
- Place in oven for about 25 minutes.
- Remove from oven, let cool for 10 minutes and cut into miniature squares.

I know you're probably thinking this sounds like a lasagna, but it's my recipe and version of a makeshift ravioli dish. Anyways, it's super yummy!

Grab a glass of white wine and enjoy!

Bestie's Truth Truffle Pasta

Serves 4-6

1/2 fettuccine noodles

1/2 cheese stuffed tortellini

truffle oil for noodles once cooked (or truffle butter)

1/2 cup butter

1 1/2 cups heavy whipping cream

2 teaspoons garlic minced

1/2 teaspoon Italian Seasoning

1/4 teaspoon pepper

1 teaspoon truffle salt

1 tablespoon truffle Seasoning

1 tablespoon onion powder

1 tablespoon garlic powder

1 cup freshly grated parmesan cheese

1 cup freshly grated pepper jack cheese

3tbsp + black truffle sauce (I use Tartufata)

Instructions

- Cook pasta as instructed on packaging.
- Once pasta is cooked, drain in colander.
- Drizzle truffle oil onto pasta and gently toss. Set aside.

- In a large skillet, add your butter and cream.
- Simmer over low heat for 2 minutes.
- Whisk in the garlic, Italian Seasoning, truffle salt, pepper, truffle seasoning, onion powder and garlic powder for one minute.
- Whisk in the parmesan cheese and pepper jack cheese until melted and finally add in your truffle sauce.
- Stir in noodles.
- Serve immediately.

While hanging out with my bestie one day, she prepared this phenomenal meal and literally brought Italy to LA with every bite. It's my recipe now, but inspired by my bestie! Lol! Life's more fun when your friends can throw down too and y'all can share recipes!

Auntie's Bow Tie Festival

2 pounds large shrimp, peeled and deveined
1 tub of lump crab meat
1 box of bow tie pasta
3 packs shredded parmesan cheese
3 bottles of Italian dressing (I pick 3 different flavors to give it more flavor)
1/2 red bell pepper, chopped
1/2 yellow bell pepper, chopped
1/2 orange bell pepper, chopped
1/2 green bell pepper, chopped
1/2 red onion, chopped

1/2 green onion, chopped
1 1/2 cups cilantro, chopped
1 medium jar of small green olives (whole not sliced)
1 cup of small grape tomatoes
Extra virgin olive oil
butter
2 teaspoons onion powder
2 teaspoons garlic powder
1 teaspoon Creole seasoning
1/4 teaspoon cayenne pepper

Instructions:

- Cook pasta as directed on packaging (al dente)

- In a large skillet, bring to a medium heat and coat bottom with olive oil and 1/4 of a stick of butter.

- Add in your large shrimp.

- Season with 1 teaspoon garlic powder and 1 teaspoon onion powder. Let sauté for about 8-10 minutes, stir occasionally.

- After shrimp is cooked, drain in colander and set aside.

- Once pasta is cooked, drain in colander and rinse with cool water. Set aside.

- In large mixing bowl, add in all of your pasta, shrimp, crab meat, bell peppers, onions, cilantro, olives, tomatoes, all your cheese, remaining onion & garlic powder, creole seasoning, cayenne pepper and 3 bottles of Italian dressings.

- Carefully stir together all ingredients with large spoon. (Make sure to be delicate with the pasta noodles to keep them whole.)

- Pour into serving bowl and refrigerate for 1 to 2 hours before serving.

This pairs to perfection with any of my meats or as a stand-alone dish!
It's soooo good, Enjoy!

Haute Jalapeño Meatballs and Pasta

1 pound ground beef
1/2 white onion minced
jalapeños, minced (I like mine very spicy,
may vary depending on how spicy you
want yours)
1/2 cup shredded pepper jack cheese
2 tablespoons onion powder
2 tablespoons garlic powder
1 tablespoon Tony Chachere's
2 teaspoons salt

2 teaspoons pepper
1 teaspoon dried basil
1 large egg
1 1/2 tablespoons oregano
1 1/2 tablespoons crush red pepper flakes
parmesan cheese
2 jars marinara sauce
spaghetti noodles
olive oil

Instructions:

- Preheat oven to 400°.

- Cook spaghetti noodles as directed on packaging.

- Once noodles are done, drain in colander. Drizzle olive oil on top and toss gently so pasta doesn't stick together.

- Lightly spray a pan or four-sided baking sheet with nonstick cooking spray.

- In a medium-size mixing bowl, combine ground beef, onions, jalapeños, pepper jack cheese, egg, basil, onion powder, garlic powder, Tony Chachere's, 1/2 tablespoon crush red pepper flakes, salt & pepper.

- Mix thoroughly until ingredients are evenly distributed. (I like to mix this with my hands)

- Shape into large meatballs using the palm of your hands.

- Place the fully shaped meatballs into the prepared baking pan.

- Sprinkle 1/2 tablespoon oregano on top of meatballs.

- Cook in the preheated oven for 25-30 minutes.

- Once meatballs have about 5 minutes left, I like to sprinkle a little more shredded pepper jack cheese on top of them and let it melt for the remaining amount of time in the oven.

- While your meatballs are cooking, in a skillet drizzle a little bit of olive oil on medium heat.

- Pour marinara sauce in and season with 1 teaspoon black pepper, 1 teaspoon salt, 1 table spoon crush red pepper, and 1 tablespoon oregano.

- Pour marinara over plated pasta and place your meatballs on top.

- Serve hot.

This pasta dish turns the heat up on your regular degular shmegular spaghetti! These Hauté Jalapeño Meatballs and marinara pasta never fail to hit the spot. Goodbye old spaghetti recipe, hello Hauté Jalapeño Meatballs!

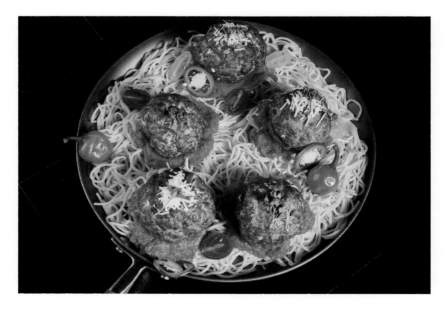

Gumbo
&
Stuff

Grouchy Gammy's Gumbo

Grouchy Gammy's Gumbo

1 jar of dark brown Roux
4 cloves of garlic (chopped)
1 bunch of GREEN Onions (chopped)
1 stalk of celery (chopped)
1 GREEN Bell pepper (chopped)
1/2 bunch of fresh parsley (chopped)
1 can diced Rotel tomatoes
2 bags of shrimp powder
Tony Chachere's Seasoning
Garlic powder
Onion powder
Gumbo fils
1 tablespoon Chicken Bouillion
2 bags of frozen or fresh shrimp
2 bags of frozen or fresh Blue crabs
2 pkgs of Chapel Hill sausage
Skinless chicken parts

Boil at least 2 gals. water (turn heat down)
Stir Roux in slowly & stir frequently
Add produce + seasoning
Add 2 or 3 more gals. of water
Turn heat up + continue to stir frequently (for about 10 to 15 mins
Add rest of other ingredients
Turn heat down to medium + stir
Cover check frequently & stir
After about 1 hr. turn heat down to low - stir
Cover & stir for about 30 mins

My Gammy's gumbo is the highlight of the holidays! This gumbo has been our holiday tradition since 1996...the year I entered the world. Every year we have a huge gumbo party on Thanksgiving Eve & Christmas Eve. My Gammy makes 2 huge pots of gumbo filled to the top with huge shrimp, sausage, chicken & crab! She would literally be in the kitchen for hours making the roux and prepping all the ingredients. When we would ask if the gumbo was ready, She would give us a loud mouth full of colorful language of which I cannot share lol! This is how she was given the name of Grouchy Gammy! We go crazy during this season. Friends & Family fill the house with gumbo bowls over flowing. Loud music, liquor and gumbo...laissez les bon temps rouler (let the good times roll). It literally is the best gumbo I have ever had in my entire freaking life! One spoon of this gumbo and I guarantee you will be hooked!

Last year my Gammy shared the recipe with me (her Silly Jilly), but gave me the short cut version for the Roux (Thank God!) I use the jar Roux (which taste just as incredible and cuts down at least an hour or more of prep time). I'm all about cutting down prep time without sacrificing taste, so the short cut version totally works for me. For some reason, I always end up with added friends when the Gumbo pots come out, but I'm cool with that...the more the merrier! After all, It really IS THE MOST WONDERFUL TIME OF THE YEAR!

Shout out to my Gammy! I will cherish this recipe now, forever & always!

Jammin' J's Jambalaya

1 1/2 tbsp. extra-virgin olive oil
1 onion, chopped
3 bell peppers, chopped
kosher salt
freshly ground black pepper
1 1/2 pound boneless skinless chicken breasts, cut into 1" pieces
1 1/2 teaspoon dried oregano
9 ounce andouille sausage, sliced
3 cloves garlic, minced
3 tablespoons tomato paste
2 1/2 cups low-sodium chicken stock
2 (10 ounce) cans rotel tomatoes
1 1/2 cups long grain rice
2 1/2 teaspoons old bay seasoning
1 1/2 pound medium shrimp, peeled and deveined
3 green onions, thinly sliced
1/4 teaspoon cayenne pepper
1 teaspoon garlic powder
1 teaspoon onion powder
1/2 teaspoon slap ya mama seasoning

Instructions:

- Cook rice according to packaging instructions.

- Once cooked, set aside.

- In a large pot, coat the bottom with olive oil over medium heat.

- Add in your onions and bell peppers and season with salt and pepper. Cook for about 5 minutes.

- Now stir in chicken and season with salt, pepper, and oregano.

- Cook until the chicken is golden, about 5-6 minutes, then stir in andouille sausage, garlic, tomato paste, slap ya mama, half a teaspoon garlic powder, half a teaspoon onion powder.

- Stir and cook until everything has a subtle crisp edge to it, about 2 minutes more.

- Add chicken broth, rotel tomatoes, rice, other half of onion powder and garlic powder,

cayenne pepper, dash of salt and 2-3 pinches of black pepper and old bay.

- Reduce heat to medium low, cover with a tight-fitting lid, and cook stirring occasionally until the rice is tender and the liquid is almost absorbed, about 20 minutes.

- In a separate pan, sauté your shrimp with olive oil, old bay seasoning and a couple pinches of black pepper.

- Add the shrimp into your pot once there's about 2 minutes left of cooking.

- Stir so everything is mixed evenly.

- Once Jambalaya is ready to be served, garnish with green onions just before serving.

Jambalaya has always been a creole staple! I couldn't complete this cookbook without my signature Jambalaya dish! Enjoy!

Crevette Fried Rice "shrimp"

1/4 red bell pepper, chopped
1/4 green bell pepper, chopped
1/4 yellow bell pepper, chopped
1/4 orange bell pepper, chopped
1/4 red onion, chopped
3 tablespoons minced Garlic
1 pound shrimp, peeled and deveined
2 bags rice (I prefer boil in bag rice)
stir fry oil
butter
soy sauce
garlic powder
onion powder
garlic salt
ground black pepper
Tony Chachere's

Instructions:

- Boil rice as instructed on packaging.

- Once boiled, set aside

- In a Wok, melt 1/2 stick of butter on medium heat

- Add in your shrimp, bell peppers, onions, 2 tablespoons minced garlic

- Season with 1 tablespoon garlic powder, 1 tablespoon onion powder, 1 teaspoon Tony Chachere's, 1 teaspoon black pepper, 1 teaspoon garlic salt

- Drizzle in your stir fry oil and let sauté for about 7 minutes.

- Add in boiled rice, 1/2 stick butter, 1 tablespoon minced garlic, 1/4 cup soy sauce, 1 teaspoon garlic powder, 1 teaspoon onion powder, 1/2 teaspoon Tony Chachere's, 1 teaspoon black pepper.

- Allow to cook for about 2 minutes, constantly stirring.

This Crevette Fried Rice is truly the perfect add on to any dish. *Warning* You may enjoy this more than the main course itself, Lol!

Crabby Crab & Sausage Rice

serves 6 to 8

2 large bags rice cooked rice
2 tubs of lump or claw crab meat (I prefer lump)
2 rolls of hot turkey breakfast sausage
1/4 red bell pepper, thinly sliced
1/4 yellow bell pepper, thinly sliced
1/4 green bell pepper, thinly sliced
1/4 red onion, chopped
2 tablespoons minced garlic
2 sticks butter
Extra virgin olive oil
1 tablespoon onion powder
1 tablespoon garlic powder
1 tablespoon garlic pepper
1 tablespoon Creole seasoning

Instructions:

- In large skillet add butter, heat on medium
- Sauté bell peppers, onions and garlic 4 to 6 minutes
- Add lump crab meat and sauté an additional 2 minutes then set aside

- In a separate skillet, cover bottom with olive oil, heat on medium heat
- Add hot turkey sausage, cook for 5 to 7 minutes or until thoroughly cooked
- Drain turkey sausage in colander
- Pour sausage into large skillet with sautéed bell peppers, onions, minced garlic, crab meat and butter
- Add 2 bags rice, stir all ingredients
- Season with garlic powder, garlic pepper, onion powder & Creole seasoning
- Slowly stir all ingredients well
- Cook on low heat for 2 to 3 minutes
- Now serve that Crabby Crab & Sausage Rice!

This rice is a whole mood by itself, but if you want something extra on your plate then pair it with Theresa Gail's Lamb chops!

There's never a morsel of rice left once this dish hits the table.
#SoFreakingGood

#4's Must Have Dressing

Cornbread Dressing

4 pkgs. Cornbread mix
Chicken Gizzards
Turkey necks
Tony Chacheres
Onion powder
Garlic powder
Thyme
2 stalks of Celery (chopped)
1 Bell pepper (chopped)
1 Bunch Green Onions (chopped)
3 cloves of garlic (chopped)
6 can of cream of Chicken
Boil Gizzards & Turkey necks with All ingredients
for about 1 1/2 hrs.
Cook Cornbread as instructed
Chop Gizzards Small, pull meat off of Turkey necks
Mix All ingredients with Cornbread
Chop 1 more stalk of celery (mix in with ingredients
Stir in 2 uncooked eggs & put in oven on 400°
for About 45 mins.

For decades, this dressing was only made twice a year, for Thanksgiving and Christmas. But because my LoveBug loved it so much, it's now on the table often! Thanks for the recipe Gammy... I think he still thinks it's mine lol!

Seafood Simmer

Serves 6 to 8

2 pounds large shrimp peeled and deveined
2 packages of crawfish
1 tub lump crabmeat
1/4 red bell pepper, chopped
1/4 green bell pepper, chopped
1/4 yellow bell pepper, chopped
1/4 red onion, chopped
2 garlic cloves, chopped
1 tablespoon minced garlic
1/4 green onion, chopped
1 pack ground shrimp

1 large can cream of mushroom
1 small can cream of mushroom
2 cans golden mushroom
1 cup seafood stock
1 stick of butter
2 tablespoons Creole seasoning
1 tablespoon onion powder
1 tablespoon garlic powder
1 tablespoon garlic pepper
1 teaspoon cayenne pepper
2 large bags cooked rice (I like Boil in Bag)

Instructions:

- In large skillet, add butter and heat on medium
- Add bell peppers, onions and garlic
- Sauté 5 to 7 minutes, then set aside
- In large sauce pot pour in all cream of mushrooms and golden mushrooms, stir until mixed well
- Add pack of ground shrimp, stir
- Pour in all of sautéed bell peppers, onions and garlic, including butter, into the large sauce pot with the soups
- Add uncooked shrimp and crawfish
- Season with Creole seasoning, onion powder, garlic powder, garlic pepper & cayenne pepper, stir well
- Cook on medium for about 12 to 15 minutes, stir occasionally mixing in shrimp & crawfish
- Stir in 1 cup seafood stock
- Stir in tub of lump crabmeat
- Turn on low heat and simmer for about 20 minutes, continue to stir occasionally

- Serve over rice

I like to top mine off with a few splashes of Louisiana hot sauce!

This is complete comfort food! A little heavy in calories, but totally worth every bite. I'll worry about working it off later! Lol

#Yummmmms

Companions

Daddy's Favorite Coleslaw

4 tablespoons spicy brown mustard
2 cup olive oil mayonnaise
4 teaspoons celery seeds
2 teaspoon onion powder
1 1/2 teaspoon kosher salt
6 tablespoons sugar
4 tablespoons apple cider vinegar
two 16 ounce bags of coleslaw mix

Instructions:

- Stir together, in a large mixing bowl, spicy brown mustard, mayonnaise, celery seeds, onion powder, salt, sugar, vinegar.
- Once ingredients are stirred together add in the bag of coleslaw mix.
- Stir until ingredients and coleslaw mix are completely evenly distributed.
- Refrigerate for about an hour before serving.
- Stir once more prior to serving.

This year on 4th of July (2020), we had our usual 4th of July spread; ribs, hamburgers, hotdogs, beans and more! For some odd reason everyone was craving coleslaw, which we never make. Everyone looked at me and I looked away as if I was trying to ignore the hint of me being voted to make it! Lol, I caved in and googled a few slaw recipes. I wasn't too impressed by especially since I have never really been a slaw eating girl. So instead I added my own touch of spicy brown mustard which drastically changed the taste! Needless to say, I have become the designated Coleslaw maker every family gathering! My dad makes sure to call me reminding me to make it prior to any family function!

Damn Daddy Potato Dish

2 sweet potatoes
2 white potatoes
2 large cartons heavy whipping cream
1 large stick butter
1/2 cup pickled jalapeños, chopped
sea salt
ground black pepper

Instructions:

- Peel potatoes using a potato peeler, then thinly slice potatoes in a wheel shape using a food slicer or a sharp knife.

- In a large casserole dish layer 1 layer of white potatoes, 1 layer of sweet potatoes, sprinkle with chopped jalapeños, lightly sprinkle with sea salt and pepper, evenly spread 8 slices of butter. Then cover layer with heavy whipping cream.

- Repeat with second layer of both potatoes, chopped jalapeños, salt and pepper, butter and cover completely with heavy whipping cream again.

- Cover dish with foil and cook on 350° for 2 1/2 hours.

- Uncover after 2/12 hours and cook an additional 30 to 40 minutes until golden brown.

Dig in and you'll be hollering Damn Daddy this is good! This dish is one of my holiday favorites! I damn near have to trip my daddy so I can get first dibs...
Hence the name, Damn Daddy!

Elote Charcoal Corn

corn on the cob
olive oil mayonnaise
chili powder
grated cotija cheese
freshly chopped cilantro
lime wedges
butter

Instructions:

- Grill corn to charcoal perfection!

- Make sure as you grill your corn you turn often to evenly charcoal the corn all around (approximately 10-15 minutes on the grill)

- Once corn is grilled to perfection, immediately lather butter all around each cob.

- Next, lather a layer of mayonnaise all over the cob followed by sprinkling chili powder, cotija and cilantro all over.

- Serve with lime wedges so you can squeeze on for taste!

This Elote Charcoal Corn is to die for! My goodness, it is worth every kernel that gets stuck in your teeth. Have floss picks near by!

Garlic Sautéed Spinach

Extra virgin olive oil
spinach
1 teaspoon minced garlic
1 garlic clove, peeled and chopped
onion powder
garlic powder
black pepper
Tony Chachere's

Instructions:

- In a skillet, drizzle olive oil on the bottom on top of medium heat.
- Add in your washed and cleaned spinach, 1 teaspoon minced garlic, 1 garlic clove, 1/4 teaspoon Tony Chachere's, 1/2 teaspoon onion powder, 1/2 teaspoon garlic powder and 1/4 teaspoon black pepper.
- Stir often so spinach doesn't burn and cooks evenly.
- (Note: Spinach wilts quickly, therefore it may seem like you're putting in a lot by piling it up in the skillet but in actuality it drastically shrinks and is not a lot at all.)
- Using tongs, gently toss the spinach so all of the unwilted leaves make contact with the bottom of the pan.
- Once all the spinach is completely wilted and has turned a bright green, it is ready to eat!

Broccolini

broccolini
Extra virgin olive oil
ground black pepper
onion powder
garlic powder
Tony Chachere's

Instructions:

- In a large skillet, coat the bottom with olive oil on medium heat.
- Add in your washed broccolini.
- Drizzle a light amount of olive oil on top of your broccolini.
- Add 1 teaspoon of onion powder, 1 teaspoon garlic powder, 1/4 teaspoon Tony Chachere's, 1/4 teaspoon black pepper.
- Toss gently.
- Allow to cook until broccolini is a bright green (about 8 minutes) tossing occasionally.
- Now this is ready to eat!

Not everyone is a fan of greens, but that's because not everyone knows how to make greens to be a fan of! These Garlic Sautéed Spinach and Broccolini recipes pair well with any and everything. Don't be surprised because you'll definitely want more!

Zesty Zucchini and Squash

8 wooden or bamboo skewers
2 zucchini
2 squash
1/2 red onions
1 red bell peppers
1 orange bell peppers
1 green bell peppers
2 garlic cloves
1/3 cup olive oil
1/8 teaspoon black pepper
1/2 teaspoon salt
1/2 teaspoon onion powder
1/2 teaspoon garlic powder
1 1/2 teaspoon dried basil
3/4 teaspoon dried oregano

Instructions:

- Cut your zucchini and squash into 1 inch slices.

- Cut your onions and bell peppers into chunks.

- Soak your wooden or bamboo skewers in warm water for about 20 minutes. (Wooden or bamboo skewers burn easily over hot grills. This will keep the skewers from cooking along with the food.)

- Preheat the grill to medium heat and lightly oil the grate.

- Now thread your zucchini, squash, onions, bell peppers, garlic cloves alternating between each onto your skewers.

- In a bowl, whisk together your olive oil, basil, oregano, salt, black pepper, onion powder and garlic powder.

- Brush the mixture over your veggies.

- Place skewers on grill. Skewers will need to be constantly turned while cooking.

- Occasionally brush olive oil mixture onto skewers as the continue to cook.

- Cook until veggies are crisp and tender.

- After about 13-15 minutes of constantly turning, skewers are completely cooked.

These skewers pair well with Baby Brudder's T-Bone Steak *(pg. 31)*
and my Le Bácon Wrapped Filet *(pg. 33)*

Fancy Filet & Crab Deviled Eggs

1 dozen of brown organic eggs, boiled
2 cooked filets or any preferred steak, thinly sliced (medium well temperature is best)
1 tub crab claw or lump crab meat
1 tablespoon dill relish
2 tablespoons Olive Oil Mayonnaise (I prefer Hellman's)
1 teaspoon Dijon mustard
1/4 teaspoon cayenne pepper
1/4 teaspoon paprika
1 teaspoon Creole seasoning
1/8 teaspoon Italian Seasoning

Instructions:

- Slice boiled eggs in half and spoon out yolk.
- Place yolks in mixing bowl along with dill relish, mayonnaise, dijon mustard and crab meat.
- Season egg mixture with Creole seasoning, paprika and cayenne pepper.
- Stir all ingredients together and place in deviled egg maker.
- Squeeze mixture from deviled egg maker to fill each egg.
- If you do not have a deviled egg maker, use a teaspoon to spoon fill each egg.

- Now, lay a slice of filet on top of each filled deviled egg.
- Sprinkle a bit of crab meat, paprika and Italian seasoning on top of steak and egg.

Oh You Fancy huh?! Now this is ready to serve!
This is a hit at every kick back! Not sure if the invitation is for me or for my
Fancy Filet & Crab Deviled Eggs... Either way my deviled eggs & I are the high-
light of every party!

Salads

Seared Scallop Salad

Serves 4-6

2 packs scallops (I prefer large but Bay scallops are just as yummy)
1 carton mixed greens
1 carton arugula
1 bottle capers
1 bottle Kalamata olives
2 lemons Sliced in a wheel shape

1 pack shredded parmesan cheese
champagne vinaigrette
olive oil
butter
1 teaspoon lemon pepper seasoning
1 teaspoon Tony Chachere's

Instructions:

- In large skillet cover bottom with olive oil and 4 slices of butter
- Stir in scallops, season with lemon pepper and Tony Chachere's
- Sauté on medium heat for 5 to 7 minutes, stir occasionally
- Remove from heat and pour in colander and set aside

- In a large salad bowl combine and toss Mixed greens and arugula
- Sprinkle in 1 bag of parmesan cheese and toss
- Add 1/2 jar of Kalamata olives
- Pour about a half of a bottle of the champagne vinaigrette over the greens and toss (add more if salad looks too dry)
- Top salad with sautéed scallops, 1/2 bottle of capers and add lemons slices around the edge of the bowl

Enjoy! This is one delish dish! If you love scallops, this is a must have salad!
No sharing off my plate...get your own!
#YummyForMyTummy

Pretty Pear Salad

———❖———

Serves 6

1 large carton of spinach
2 pears sliced thinly in wheel slices
1 cup blue cheese crumbles
1 cup gorgonzola crumbles
1 cup thinly sliced red onion
1 bottle of champagne vinaigrette

Instructions:

- In large salad bowl add 1/2 carton spinach, 1/2 cup blue cheese, 1/2 cup gorgonzola cheese and 1/2 cup thinly sliced onion

- Toss in 1/4 cup champagne vinaigrette

- Lightly mix ingredients

- Top with 6 slices of pears

- Layer with remaining spinach, 6 slices of pears, 1/2 cup blue cheese, 1/2 cup gorgonzola cheese and 1/2 cup thinly sliced onion

- Drizzle top with 1/4 cup champagne vinaigrette

- Serve immediately

- (If not serving immediately prepare as directed but do not add champagne vinaigrette.

- Add champagne vinaigrette when ready to serve)

- Also amazing with crumbled bacon on top!

#soprettyandsodelicious
This salad is great solo or coupled with Fish, Chicken, Beef or Pork and of course
a generous pour of wine!

Shrimpy Salad

Serves 6-8

2 pounds large shrimp peeled and deveined
1 pound small shrimp peeled and deveined
1 dozen jumbo prawns head and shell on
(optional-used for presentation)
1 carton spinach
1 carton arugula
1 1/2 cups grape tomatoes
1 cup red grapes, sliced in half

1 1/2 cups burrata cheese
1/2 dozen boiled eggs sliced in 1/2
1 bottle balsamic vinaigrette
olive oil
butter
1 teaspoon Slap ya Mama Creole seasoning
1 teaspoon garlic powder

Instructions:

- In large skillet cover bottom with olive oil and 1/2 stick of butter
- Pre heat on medium high until warm
- Add large shrimp and small shrimp, season with Slap yo Mama Creole seasoning and garlic powder
- Sauté on medium for 10 to 12 minutes or until shrimp is thoroughly cooked
- Pour into colander and set aside
- Place large skillet on medium heat and cover bottom with olive oil
- Once bottom of skillet is warm, add large prawns with head and shell on
- Toss in olive oil and stir
- Cook for 8 to 10 minutes
- Remove prawns from skillet and set aside

- In large salad bowl combine spinach and arugula
- Add 1 cup burrata cheese

- 1 cup grape tomatoes
- 1/2 cup sliced red grapes
- Toss all ingredients
- Add 1/2 bottle balsamic vinaigrette, toss (add more if needed)
- Cover top with large and small shrimp
- Place 2 rows of large prawns to one side of bowl with heads tilted up
- Place 2 rows of sliced boiled eggs to opposite side of bowl.
- Sprinkle top with remaining grapes, tomatoes and burrata cheese
- Drizzle with balsamic vinaigrette
- Serve immediately
- (If not serving immediately prepare as directed but do not toss with balsamic vinaigrette until ready to serve.
- Add balsamic to individual servings)

#tasteasgoodasitlooks
There is nothing better than a great salad and this salad should win an award
for best looks and most delicious!
Enjoy

It's
5 o'clock
Somewhere

Lemon Drop Your Panties!

2 ounces citron vodka
1/2 ounce triple sec
1 ounce simple syrup
1 ounce fresh lemon juice
3/4 ounce (1 1/2 tablespoons) Cointreau or triple sec
garnish: sugar rim or lemon sugar

- Coat the rim of a cocktail glass with sugar or lemon sugar and set aside (do this a few minutes ahead of time so the sugar can dry and adhere well to glass).
- Add all the ingredients into a shaker with ice.
- Shake. Pour. Sip. And the name speaks for itself. Whatever happens when you drink this lemon drop, stays between you and this lemon drop! HA!

Dirty Martini

My traditional dirty vodka martini....shaken (NOT STIRRED) served with stuffed green olives or blue cheese olives. This dirty martini is one of the best classic cocktails ever!

2 1/2 ounces vodka (or gin)
1/4 ounce dry vermouth
1/4 to 1/2 ounce olive juice or olive brine
garnish with 3 olives on a skewer/toothpick

- In a shaker, fill with ice, pour vodka, dry vermouth, and olive juice. Shake for approximately 30 seconds. Pour in martini glass. Garnish with olives on skewer or toothpick. ENJOY!

J Mo's Mojito

2 oz fresh lime juice
approx. 10 fresh mint leaves
2 oz of vodka or gin (I prefer vodka)
4 ounces ginger beer
garnish: fresh lime wedges or slices, fresh mint sprigs
splash of cranberry juice (optional)

- Muddle the mint in with the lime juice.
- Then add in some ice cubes, vodka and ginger beer.
- Top it off with some extra mint and lime slices for garnish!
- Add a splash of cranberry juice (it's a creole thang)

Rose Sangria

1 bottle rosé
1/2 cup Pom Wonderful pomegranate juice
3 tablespoons Grand Marnier
2 tablespoon Cognac
1/4 cup lemon juice (2 to 3 lemons)
1/3 cup sugar
fresh raspberries, strawberries, pineapples,
and and star fruit.

- Combine all juices and sugar in a pitcher on little ice. Stir in raspberries, strawberries and plums. Refrigerate.
- When ready to serve, pour the sangria over ice.
- Garnish with starfruit, raspberries and/or pineapple slice.

Grand Gold Margarita

1 oz tequila
1 of Grand Marnier
0.5 oz fresh lime juice
limes for garnish
Tajin Seasoning

- Rub rim of class with lime. Dip rim in Tajin.
- Mix all liquids in shaker with ice
- Add ice to glass
- Pour mix in margarita glass

Delicioso!!

Strawberry Elderflower Spritzer

1 cup prosecco or sparkling white wine, chilled
1/4 cup pomegranate juice
1/4 cup Elderflower liqueur such as St. Germain
1 cup club soda
1/2 cup strawberries
mint leaves
blueberries
lime slices

- Mix liquids. Do not shake. Stir.
- Add fruit and garnish with mint and lime slice.